THE SUNDERLAND FLYING BOAT QUEEN

VOLUME 2

JOHN EVANS

FOREWORD

Wing Commander Guy Van der Kiste DSO OBE
(ex 210, 201 ann 88 Squadrons, RAF)

Although I had always wanted to get onto 'boats, never in my wildest dreams did I expect that I would have the good fortune to become a Sunderland pilot, and eventually command two squadrons of them.

In June, 1939, I was sent on a flying-boat conversion course at Calshot, starting on Stranraers, and then Singapores, and in July I was posted to 210 Squadron at Pembroke Dock. Here, for the first time, I saw a Sunderland at close quarters. I was amazed how enormous it was; about as big as six double-decker buses, and yet able to be handled in the air by one man.

That August I was given my own 'boat, L5798, and crew and we stayed together until the squadron was re-equipped with Catalinas in April, 1941. In those pre planned-maintenance days we took great pride in our own aircraft, adding little personal touches to them. Together we carried out 150 sorties and although on occasions, owing to damage or maintenance work, we had to fly other 'boats, 'ole 98' as we affectionately called her, was undoubtedly the best Sunderland we built.

Converting to Catalinas, after the space and comfort we had previously enjoyed, was an awful wrench, and somehow we never built up the same rapport with them.

After a break between tours I was given 201 Squadron, still equipped with Sunderlands, at Castle Archdale, and we moved to Pembroke Dock for D-Day.

Two years later I was to command 88 Squadron in Hong Kong, where Sunderlands were being used in a transport role, flying to Japan.

Then, on 3rd December, 1947, I had my last flight on one of these wonderful aircraft, and so said farewell to a very happy period of my service life.

With the remorseless march of time, the operation of flying-boats became economically unacceptable as landplanes with powerful jet engines needed smaller runways, and the expense of maintaining water bases was no longer a viable proposition.

Now, like the dinosaur, flying-boats have been relegated to museum pieces but we old 'webfooted' types are delighted that John Evans has produced another fine volume on the Sunderland which will rekindle our memories of those golden years.

R. E. G. Van der Kiste DSO OBE
Wing Commander, RAF South Brent, Devon, March 1993.

Best boat of all... Sunderland I L5798, Wing Commander Guy Van der Kiste's own aircraft when on 210 Squadron. He is in the cockpit as 'ole 98' taxies past. First flown on 1st September, 1939, L5798 spent over 18 months with 210 Squadron before joining 201 Squadron in April, 1941. It transferred to 204 Squadron in July, 1941, and flew many operations over the South Atlantic. This veteran Sunderland survived everything except the weather, being damaged in a gale at Gibraltar in September, 1943. It was flown back to Calshot and scrapped.

IMPERIAL WAR MUSEUM CH842

INTRODUCTION

The Short Sunderland remains one of the most famous of all British military aircraft. While many lesser types have long been forgotten, the Sunderland is still instantly remembered and recognised, epitomising the very finest in flying-boat design, grace and power.

The Sunderland's first flight – on 16th October, 1937 – was the beginning of an unique chapter in British aviation history which encompassed both war and peace, and by the time the Sunderland retired from service in the Royal Air Force in 1959, it had served its country for a then unequalled 21 years.

This was not the end of the story for this 'Queen of the Flying-Boats' soldiered on with other nations until the middle 1960s, remarkable testimony of the versatility of a supreme design which originated back in 1933.

And the story continues into the 1990s with just one of the famous breed still in flying order – but soon to leave British shores for the last time for a new home in the USA.

For its day, the Sunderland was a huge machine. When it entered service it was by far the largest aircraft ever used by the Royal Air Force, yet it was so docile and forgiving that it could be flown by one man.

In war and peace Sunderlands endeared themselves to those who flew them, and those who serviced them, in many parts of the world. They carried out a multitude of tasks from the Arctic north to the southern tip of Africa.

It was the Air Ministry's Specification R.2/33 of November, 1933, which resulted in the Sunderland – specifying a long-range, four-engined, general purpose flying-boat for the RAF. A monoplane was not actually dictated, but the resulting design from the famous Shorts Company was for a streamlined high wing monoplane. It looked right, it required very little modification before entering service, and it was to prove itself over and over again as a winner.

The Sunderland's entry into RAF service in 1938 came at a time of high tension, as the war clouds darkened over Europe. That it would be called to war was never in doubt, and the aircraft was one of the very few types which served throughout the six years of the conflict.

It proved itself a worthy warrior in all theatres of operations; a worthy opponent for the Luftwaffe in aerial battles over the Bay of Biscay, and a worthy hunter of the 'Sea Wolves', the German U-Boats whose operations threatened to cripple Britain's ability to wage war.

The Sunderland was initially powered by Bristol Pegasus radial engines which, though over taxed and often at emergency power settings, gave splendid service. Late in the war it was the 'marriage' of the Sunderland airframe with the more powerful and very trusty American Pratt and Whitney power plants that gave the aircraft a new lease of life, extending well into the jet age.

After its RAF days the Sunderland continued in service with the French Navy and the Royal New Zealand Air Force. The South African Air Force, too, were operators of the type for several years. And in wartime men of many nations crewed and serviced this majestic 'queen'.

In all, 749 Sunderlands were built between 1937 and 1946, the main Shorts factory at Rochester, Kent, being joined in wartime by another Shorts factory at Windermere, the Short and Harland works in Belfast and Blackburns at Dumbarton, all producing Sunderlands.

Sadly, very little regard was given, even in the late 1950s, to preservation of examples of our aviation heritage so today there are very few of this superb British type – the 'Queen of the Flying-Boats' – remaining for new generations to behold and marvel at.

Flying-boats proved their worth in protecting Britain's sovereignty as an island nation which is dependent on its maritime trade. And had the Sunderland not been designed – or had not proved itself to be such a winner – Britain would conceivably have found itself in even more peril in those dark days of World War II.

This book is the second in a series of three and was first published in 1993. It and its sister volumes reflect the multitude of roles that Sunderlands were called upon to carry out during nearly 30 years of active service all over the world.

I. FIRST LADY

Workhorse... While so many of its sisters went to war, K4774 soldiered on for years as a trials workhorse, serving in this role at MAEE Helensburgh. Here it was involved in tests which ultimately led to the faired main step introduced on Mark III Sunderlands. The 'end' of K4774 is unclear – it may well have made its last flight in February, 1942, when damaged by a depth charge exploding on impact. This photograph was taken at Helensburgh and shows two airmen by the port midship gun position, a feature of Mark I and early Mark II Sunderlands. In the background is the unique twin-finned Saro Lerwick flyingboat, an experimental development of a type which should have served alongside Sunderlands but which proved an absolute disaster.

GROUP CAPTAIN E. MADGER via BILL MORTIMER

Postcard... Dubbed 'The Flying Battleship', this postcard of the Sunderland prototype, K4774, was eagerly sought after by aviation collectors in the months running up to World War II. The Sunderland – a massive four engined monster – represented the pinnacle of British aviation achievement and was by far the largest aircraft in the inventory of the Royal Air Force. This photograph is from a 'Valentine's' postcard and the outline of the aircraft has been re-touched, making it look somewhat unreal. There was nothing though 'unreal' about the first of the many Sunderlands to grace the waters and the air in a career which was to span nearly 30 years in military terms, and even longer in civilian guises, up to the 1990s.

SQUADRON LEADER PETER SEYMOUR COLLECTION via DR ARTHUR BANKS

Modifications... K4774 first flew on 16th October, 1937, at the hands of John Parker, and powered temporarily by Bristol Pegasus X engines, each of 950hp. Two flights totalling 45 minutes were followed by further flights on the 21st and 28th before the prototype returned to Shorts No.3 Shop at Rochester for the wings to have a 4½ degree sweepback and modifications to be made to the main step. These were brought about by late changes to the design to incorporate turrets nose and tail, and a consequent shift in the centre of gravity. At the same time 1010hp Pegasus XXIIs were installed. Modifications took until the following March and Parker resumed flight tests on the 7th, these being completed in a month, and K4774 began its next important chapter by being handed over to the Marine Aircraft Experimental Establishment at Felixstowe. It is seen here soon after arrival at MAEE, majestically poised on its beaching gear. A bicycle rests against the port beaching leg proving that for all its power and glory, the Sunderland flying-boat did not have all the advantages!

BILL SIMPSON

First of many... L2158, the first production Sunderland, rides regally at its mooring, doubtless soon after its initial flight at the hands of John Parker on 21st April, 1938. Various test flights followed, including one on 9th May when Parker took the aircraft to 13,000 feet. Auto-pilot and turret tests were satisfactorily completed at Rochester before L2158 departed for MAEE at Felixstowe in June. It was to remain in MAEE's hands for a long period before finally becoming a 'fully fledged' operational 'boat with 204 Squadron at Bathurst. It met its end on 17th August, 1942, when ships in the convoy it was protecting saw the Sunderland crash and the depth charges aboard explode. In 204's service L2158 carried a full array of ASV aerials and the code letters KG-M.

REAL PHOTOGRAPHS/MAP

Royal send-off... N9021 on the Kalafrana, Malta, slipway, April, 1939. The aircraft was then on 202 Squadron's 'books' but it was to be a short-lived thing for 202 was destined for other types. First flown on 14th March, N9021 had royal watchers for the King and Queen were visiting Shorts at Rochester that day. N9021 had a short but nomadic existence amongst the squadrons, serving with 202, 228 and 204 Squadrons before transferring to 201 in October, 1940. Before the year was out N9021 had become a casualty, capsizing and sinking at Sullom Voe on 15th December.

via ANDY THOMAS

Peggy power... The faithful Bristol Pegasus engine which powered all the Mark I, II and III Sunderlands. Developing just over 1000 hp, the Peggies were called upon to perform under wartime conditions at ratings far above that specified, and gave sterling service.

SHORT BROTHERS R8902545, via JOHN PRITCHARD

Hot task... In sweltering heat, personnel from 228 Squadron change an engine on the water of an Egyptian lake, August, 1939. Skill, training, patience, improvisation and a bit of luck were all requirements for the task in hand.

BOB JONES

Med maiden... One of 228 Squadron's early 'boats, N9025, up on the Imperial Airways slipway at Alexandria in the summer of 1939. Soon after war was declared N9025 helped make a bit of aviation history, joining in the rescue of the crew of the merchantman *Kensington Court* which was torpedoed 100 miles south-west of the Bishop Rock. Flight Lieutenant Thurston Smith and crew in N9025, along with 204 Squadron's L5802, skippered by Flight Lieutenant Jackie Barrett, landed and picked up all 34 crew. This rescue resulted in DFC awards for Smith and Barrett. Italian intervention in the Mediterranean saw 228 Squadron return to warmer climes and N9025 was lost on 6th August, 1940, when Smith and his crew were shot down by an Italian Fiat CR 42. This was the beginning of a long period of captivity for the Sunderland crew.

GROUP CAPTAIN DAVID BEVAN-JOHN

All is calm... Soaking up the Mediterranean sun in the last pre-war summer is N6133, seen at Nelson's Island, Aboukir Bay. The first of a batch of three Sunderlands, N6133 joined 228 Squadron early in 1939, moving to 201 Squadron at Sullom Voe soon after the squadron re-equipped with Sunderlands in May, 1940. N6133 became another statistic of the air-sea war when it went missing on patrol on 9th July, 1940.

GROUP CAPTAIN DAVID BEVAN-JOHN

Midships... Vigilance to both port and starboard from the midships gun positions. Mark Is and early Mark IIs had these positions, later replaced by a FN7 twin-gun turret. Flying helmets and balaclavas were vital headgear against the elements.

AUTHOR'S COLLECTION

Taking shape... Short Brothers workmen pose on and around one of the first of the new breed as it nears completion in the Rochester works.

HENRY ROLFE

Cliffs queen... Over England's famous South Coast cliffs, L2165 of 210 Squadron flies the flag, Summer 1939. This aircraft made Pembroke Dock history by flying the first wartime patrol on 3rd September. Just 15 days later L2165 was to crash in the Milford Haven Waterway after running out of fuel on a night return from patrol.

MRS NANCY OWEN

Selangor... An early in-flight shot of L2160 which first flew on 18th May, 1938. L2160 joined 230 Squadron at Seletar and was one of three aircraft specially 'christened' in honour of the Sultans from the Federated Malay States who contributed £300,000 for the Sunderlands' purchase. L2160 was named Selangor on 19th October, 1938. After lengthy service with 230 Squadron L2160 returned to the UK and eventually became a ground instructional airframe, No 3372M. Its final fate is unrecorded.

MRS GWENETH TEESDALE

11

In its element... One of the first Sunderlands creams up the surface of the water as the power is increased – an impressive sight.

J. L. WATSON

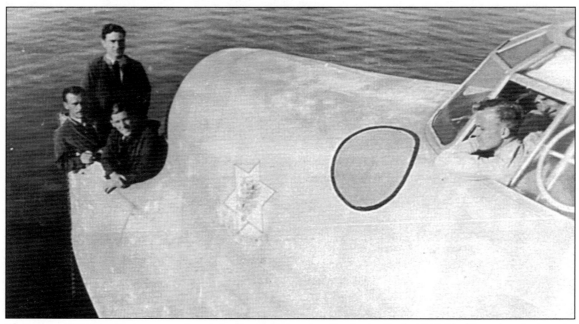

Up front... 210 Squadron personnel pose for the cameraman at Pembroke Dock, 1939. The Squadron Badge of a griffin in a six-pointed star is displayed prominently while just below the cockpit is what is thought to be a gas detecting panel, coloured orange with a black outline.

MRS ANNA McCORRY

Ready for war... X for X-Ray, N9023, of 228 Squadron, awaits the call at Alexandria Harbour, August 1939. N9023 served with 228 from April 1939, until June 1940. When with 204 Squadron based at Reykjavik, it crashed into an Icelandic hill on 24th April, 1941.

EDGAR MORGAN

VGOs... Another view of the midships gun positions as LAC C. Fry and AC J. Tanner of 210 Squadron pose with their single Vickers gas operated K guns. The metal windshields standing proud deflected some of the slipstream, but 'draughty' was something of an understatement!

FRED THOMAS

III. WAR WINGS

Taking the waters... With the starboard outer already fired up T9041 of 204 Squadron takes to the waters. Judging by the hut behind, the location is definitely West African! Coded KG-V, T9041 joined 204 in September 1941, after spells with 210, 95 and 201 Squadrons. An Atlantic patrol on 28th June, 1942, was to be T9041's last. It was forced to ditch after all the engines failed and most of the crew were picked up from the water two days later. 204 Squadron, pre-war based at Mount Batten, was later stationed in the Shetlands and then Iceland. In 1941 the Squadron headed for the warmth of West Africa, being ever present at places like Bathurst, Jui and Port Etienne.

MRS M. C. MORTON

Beached... Handsomely sitting on its beaching gear at Mount Batten, Rochester-built Mark II W3985 waits patiently for a return to the water and to operations. Carrying the RB-T code combination of 10 Squadron, RAAF, W3985 was one of 43 Mark IIs built. It joined 10 Squadron in August 1941, and exactly two years later became another casualty of the air battle over the Bay of Biscay, being shot down by the Luftwaffe on 18th August, 1943.

BILL STARK

Attack!... Two graphic photographs taken during the attack by Sunderland W4030 'H' of 10 Squadron, RAAF, on U-243, 8th July, 1944. The attack, by Flight Lieutenant Bill Tilley and crew, sent the Type VIIC U-Boat to the bottom, 39 of its crew being rescued by a Canadian escort vessel. A Rochester built Mark III, W4030 served with 202, 119 and 10 Squadrons. It was damaged in an accident in September, 1944, and although flown to Wig Bay was found to be beyond economic repair, being struck off RAF Charge. *BILL TILLEY*

Death plume... Exploding depth charges send a huge plume of water skywards during the joint attack on U-563, a Type VIIC U-Boat, on 31st May, 1943. First attacked by a RAF Halifax, U-563 later received the undivided attentions of Sunderlands DV969 'E' of 10 Squadron, RAAF, and DD838 'X' of 228 Squadron. Flight Lieutenant Max Mainprize and his Australian crew's first attack is seen here, and Flying Officer Bill French and his 228 crew provided the 'coup de grace'. U-563 was a veteran of eight war cruises, and its successes had included the sinking of *HMS Cossack*, the destroyer which became famous for rescuing prisoners from the German tanker *Altmark* in 1940. *CRAWFORD BLACK*

Hatch watch... A hand-held camera is operated from a waist hatch of a patrolling Sunderland.
GROUP CAPTAIN TOM HARVEY

Formal... Newly arrived CO Wing Commander D. Michell with officers and men of 204 Squadron pose for a formal photograph at Jui, Freetown, West Africa, early 1945. An ASV equipped Sunderland, propeller blades pointing skywards, is an impressive backcloth. 204 Squadron spent four years in West Africa, finally disbanding in June, 1945.

W. DAVIS

Last Patrol... Smiling crewmen of 422 Squadron, RCAF, set out for their last ops trip from Pembroke Dock, 2nd June, 1945. Flight Lieutenant Duclos and crew in ML773 escorted the liner *Louis Pasteur*.

VIC KELLY

African warriors... Over 130 personnel of No 95 Squadron pose for an official squadron group at Bathurst, November 1944. Formed from a detachment of 210 Squadron at Oban in January 1941, 95 Squadron served continuously in West African locations until the war's end.

MRS R. MIDDLETON / PHILIP CHRISTOPHER / IAN PATON

Lakes Lady... Power and grace as DP176 set off on a test flight from Windermere. The first of 35 Sunderlands built in the beautiful setting of England's Lakeland, DP176 was to have a short career. It was issued to 119 Squadron in October, 1942, and carried the individual letter 'D'. It sank on 15th April, 1943, in the same month that 119 was disbanded, its aircraft being allocated to other units.

MALCOLM WARNER via DR ARTHUR BANKS

Factory fresh... Choppy water trials by new Mark III EJ164 soon after its launching at Shorts' Belfast factory. EJ164 was set for African skies, being flown out to join No 270 Squadron at Apapa, Nigeria, in February, 1944. It did not survive the war, having to ditch in the South Atlantic on 3rd October, 1944.

SHORT BROTHERS J.3.583C

Up top... John Davies, an RAF air gunner with 461 Squadron, RAAF, poses in the mid-upper Frazer Nash FN7 turret at Pembroke Dock, August 1942. The aircraft is most likely T9114 which achieved lasting fame the following May when it made a successful forced landing on Angle Airfield, the fighter station near Pembroke Dock.

JOHN DAVIES

Night hunter... The unique black painted JM673, a Mark III operated by 230 Squadron on anti-shipping operations from Koggala, Ceylon. JM673, Rochester built, was the personal aircraft of 230's CO, Wing Commander Dundas Bednall. Later on, JM673 disappeared on an operational flight on 28th November, 1944.
WING COMMANDER DUNDAS BEDNALL

◁

Icelandic interlude... NCO crewmen of 228 Squadron line up in the Reykjavik snow of January, 1943, while their 'mount', DV977, is tucked up in a hangar. DV977 was waiting a replacement engine and the crew kicked their heels for several weeks before finally returning to warmer latitudes. DV977 – code letter Y-York – was not to last long after its return, being shot down by Junkers Ju88s over the Bay of Biscay on 12th July, 1943. The airmen pictured are (L to R): Sergeants Shepherd, Doug Kneale, Brown, Sandy Peters (RNZAF), Taft Goodwin and Bob Watt (RNZAF).
DOUG KNEALE

▷

What a catch!... Fishy business from the tail end of a 461 Squadron Sunderland at Pembroke Dock. Perhaps the quarry was a U-Boat, judging by the size of the bait!
BERT TYLER

PoW flights... Flying Officer Alexander and crew of 205 Squadron line up at Koggala, Ceylon, mid 1945, with Mark V ML800 dominating the background. This crew had brought another Mark V, PP129, out from the UK. The war in the Far East ended in August but Alexander and crew flew many hours in the following two months evacuating former prisoners-of-war from Singapore to Ceylon. ML800 was not their 'boat but belonged to 230 Squadron. After its time out east, ML800 appears to have been kept in UK storage until being sold to the French Navy in July, 1957. In its naval role it served until being struck off charge in December, 1960.

GEORGE O'NEILL

Iced up... The last winter of the war saw some harsh weather conditions. At Castle Archdale, Northern Ireland base of 201 RAF and 423 RCAF Squadrons, the lake ice froze, almost providing a platform to walk out to the moored Sunderlands. This Pegasus engined Sunderland, with radar housings under each wingtip, is a Mark IIIA carrying the new 9cm ASV VIc radar. This new radar fit did not require the lattice work of aerials as on earlier equipment.

RORY O'NEILL

Tondelayo... Preparing for take-off at Jui, West Africa, 490 Squadron's R-Roger is probably EJ165, a Short and Harland built Mark III. Named 'Tondelayo', EJ165 at one time carried a drawing of an African maiden below the cockpit, port side. EJ165 returned to the UK after the war and remained in storage until sold as scrap in 1947.

JOHN WHITBREAD

New codes... Bearing traces of its 10 Squadron, RAAF, ancestry, Mark I N9050 is prepared for its role at Freetown, West Africa, one of the new 95 Squadron's early equipment. N9050, Rochester built, joined 210 Squadron in October, 1939, moving swiftly to 10 Squadron, the Australian manned unit then forming up. Here it carried 10's famous 'RB' codes. It spent much of its operational life in West Africa, surviving a forced landing near Bathurst in April, 1941, after engine failure. The aircraft drifted before running aground, but was repaired. N9050 returned to the UK in 1943, and did a training stint at Alness before being struck off charge in July, 1944.

WING COMMANDER STAN BAGGOTT
via ANDY THOMAS

Under tow... A caterpillar tractor provides the power as ML877 is brought up the Pembroke Dock slipway. This Dumbarton built Mark III carries the codes 1-G and the photograph sets something of a poser for historians. Originally allocated to 228 Squadron in April, 1944, ML877 was transferred to 422 Squadron, RCAF, also at Pembroke Dock, later in the year, taking on the letter 'G'. By then Sunderland squadrons had dispensed with the numbers allocated at each flying-boat station in favour of new code combinations, 422 receiving 'DG'. Yet the photograph shows 'G' still carrying the figure 1 – most confusing as 228 Squadron is known to have been carried '1' in 1943/44. After a long period of storage post-war – and uprating as a Mark V – ML877 took up new colours with the French Navy in 1952, serving until being struck off charge in January, 1959.

CHRIS ASHWORTH COLLECTION

Skipper's view... Flight Lieutenant Guy Van der Kiste of 210 Squadron keeps a watchful eye from the cockpit of a Mark I Sunderland. This photograph appeared in an April, 1941, issue of *The Aeroplane*, required reading for all those with an aviation interest during the war years.

WING COMMANDER GUY VAN DER KISTE

What's cooking?... The tidy galley of Sunderland Mark I P9623 of 210 Squadron. Chef of the day is Fred Thomas, who is also the washer-upper! According to an April, 1941, issue of *The Aeroplane* "...the kitchen can produce an excellent meal". Sunderland crewmen will concur with that!

FRED THOMAS

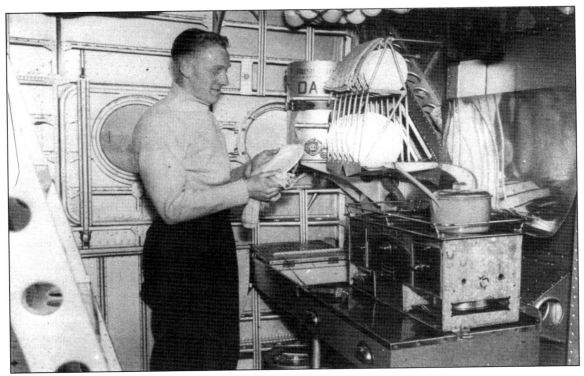

House boat... This hut, seen at Port Etienne, Mauretania, plainly shows its origins – part of the hull of a Sunderland which crashed there in 1943.

GEORGE STRATTON

Pigeon power... The SOS message slip carried on every Sunderland, along with a brace of very live pigeons. In the event of ditching far out at sea the crew could resort to pigeon power to bring help. Life or death sometimes depended on big hearted pigeons.

TREVOR ROSSITER

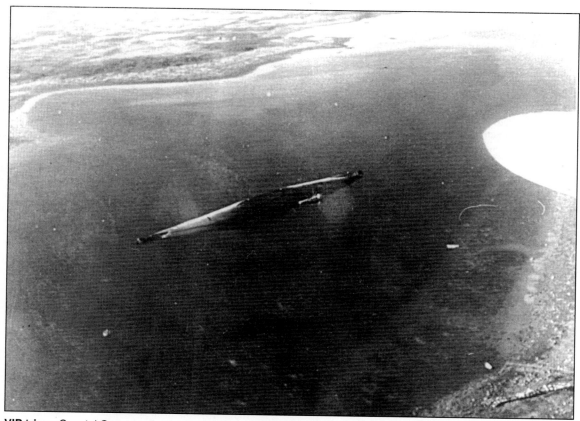

VIP trip... Coastal Command's view of Bomber Command's handiwork – the German battleship *Tirpitz* capsized in Tromso Fiord, Norway, September 1945. Flying PP112, Flight Lieutenant Brian Landers and crew from 201 Squadron flew from Sullom Voe with VIP passengers, Air Vice-Marshal Philip Mackworth of Coastal Command Headquarters and Wing Commander J. B. Tait, the former CO of 617 'Dambusters' Squadron who led the three raids against the huge warship.

BRIAN LANDERS

Big friend, little friend... The massive bulk of Sunderland III W4024 dwarfs another supreme British design, the Spitfire, at Gibraltar, August 1942. The Spitfire was destined for Malta; the Sunderland was then on 202 Squadron's roll and carries the codes AX-N. It soon transferred to 119 Squadron, moving on to 10 Squadron, RAAF, in April 1943, and spent over at year at Mount Batten. Its operational days over, W4024 languished at 57 MU, Wig Bay, until long after the war, finally being reduced to scrap in 1947.

PHIL SMITH

Hive of activity... N9022 is prepared for its next patrol with 210 Squadron. Probably pictured at Oban, it carries 210's 'DA' codes. Taken on charge by 210 in March, 1939, this aircraft had a spell with 204 Squadron before returning to 210 soon after the war started. It was written off in a crash off Oban on 27th December, 1940.

AIR MARSHAL SIR ROBERT CRAVEN

Up slip... In a remarkable experiment at Pembroke Dock in March, 1943, Sunderland W6075 was taxied up the slipway under its own power. In the capable hands of experienced pilot Flight Lieutenant Derek Martin – CO of 308 Ferry Training Unit – the experiment proved successful. However, in less experienced hands the airframe could have been stressed by even a slight deviation off line. Belfast-built W6075 went, days later, to the mainly Norwegian manned 330 Squadron, newly equipped with Sunderlands. Its time with 330 was short, being written off after a heavy landing on 12th July.

WING COMMANDER DEREK MARTIN

Backdrop... Blackburn built Mark III W6006 'G' provides a pleasant backdrop in this peaceful scene at Lough Erne. But G-George was to see plenty of action in its time, mostly with 423 Squadron, RCAF. While on convoy patrol on 12th May, 1943, Flight Lieutenant John Musgrave and crew sighted U-456 which had already been damaged the day before by air attack. When the U-Boat dived two depth charges were dropped, and naval escorts joined in the hunt. U-456 – on its second Atlantic patrol and with five ships to its credit – was shared by the 423 crew and the escorts.

GROUP CAPTAIN TOM HARVEY

Censored... The censor's hand has attempted to remove the evidence of ML876's underwing radar housing, in case the photo fell into 'wrong hands'. Blackburn built ML876 carries the NS-O combination of 201 Squadron and is seen at Pembroke Dock in 1944. Unlike so many of its companions ML876 was to have an interesting post-war civilian career. Retaining its Pegasus engines and Mark III status, ML876 underwent conversion at Queen's Island, Belfast, in 1946, fitted out for 45 passengers but retaining nose and tail turret fairings. Registered initially G-AGWX it briefly became LV-AAS in Argentina before transferring to the Uruguayian company CAUSA as CX-AKF.

IVOR WILES

Stickleback... Carrying a full array of ASV aerials, DV960 is seen on patrol when with 461 Squadron, RAAF. It carries the individual letter 'H' and the figure 2 which was allocated in the mid-war period to 461 Squadron at Pembroke Dock. DV960 had a charmed life, surviving three minor non-operational incidents including parting from its tail trolley during a maintenance period. When with 131 Operational Training Unit at Killadeas in November, 1944, DV960 ran into rocks after the pilot had to throttle back on take-off after noting that the pitot head cover had not been removed. Its wartime job done, DV960 was struck off charge in May, 1945.

JOHN HINXMAN

Ashore and afloat... Sunderlands at Jui, Sierre Leone, West Africa, a base used by 95, 204 and 490 RNZAF Squadrons for their maritime 'beat' of the South Atlantic. Conditions for the long suffering flying-boat personnel could best be described as 'basic' and maintaining Sunderlands in such far-flung locations taxed the ingenuity – and humour – of even the most stoical!

WING COMMANDER VINCE FURLONG

Author's crew... Pilot Officer Ivan Southall, RAAF, and his crew after their part in the sinking of U-385 on 11th August, 1944. Flying ML741 'P' of 461 Squadron, from Pembroke Dock, Southall and crew disabled the U-Boat in a copybook night attack and the submarine was later finished off by naval escorts. The snorkel-equipped U-385, on its second war cruise, was only two days into its patrol when attacked. Southall was awarded the DFC and in the mid-1950s wrote a splendid account of 461 Squadron, RAAF, entitled *They Shall Not Pass Unseen*. It remains one of the best accounts of wartime flying.

SQUADRON LEADER KEN FIELD

For the scrapbook... Against a leafy backdrop at Pembroke Dock officers of 201 Squadron line up for an informal photograph in 1944. Only some have been identified. Back row (L-R): ? ; ? ; 'Doc' Linehan (MO); Ernest William Lowe (pilot); ? ; ? ; ? ; Harding (nav); Ivor Wiles (nav). Front row (L-R): Harry Holt (pilot); Danny McGregor (pilot); Ian Riddell (nav); Harrison (nav); Les Baveystock (pilot); 'Red' McCready (pilot); 'Buster' Barnes (pilot); Dooley (nav); Hayes-James (Gunnery Officer). Flight Lieutenant Les Baveystock won 201's only DSO of the war, and a double DFC, while with the squadron, to add to a DFM won earlier in Bomber Command.

BRIAN LANDERS / IVOR WILES

Last patrol II... The last operational sortie by 461 Squadron, RAAF, and by an all-Australian crew in the UK, was made by the 13-man team, June 1945, all but one of whom have been identified. Back row (L-R): John Dick, 'Tubby' Allen, Rick Hannam, Ray Dunning, Roy Ganaway, Lloyd Lott, Ken May. Front row includes Tony Miller (captain), Dick Lucas, 'Porg' McNamara, 'Blue' Thompson (Gunnery Leader) and Reg Kempe.

J. E. NIXON

Seasonal... 230 Squadron's seasonal greetings card from Ceylon for the last Christmas of the war. Christmas trees, bells, palm trees... and a Sunderland!

S. J. MAXWELL

Kiwi... 490 Squadron's P-Peter taxiing by at Jui, Freetown, West Africa. This may be ML852, a Mark III built by Blackburn's at Dumbarton. Taken on charge by 490 in May, 1944, ML852 survived for just a few weeks. Following engine failure it ditched and sank off Cape St Mary on 14th July. No 490 Squadron was the only wartime Royal New Zealand Air Force flying-boat squadron, forming in March, 1943, and disbanding at Jui on 1st August, 1945.

HAROLD MARTIN

Land and sea... RAF Station Koggala in Ceylon served both landplanes and flying-boats. Five Sunderlands lie at moorings, probably from 230 Squadron which spent 15 months of the war here.

G. COLE

Composite... A dramatic view of a submarine attack by RB-A of 10 Squadron, RAAF. The photograph is most certainly a composite conjured up in the darkroom to reflect the successful attack by W4019 on the Italian *Luigi Torelli* on 7th June, 1942. Already damaged by a Wellington three days earlier, the Italian U-Boat was rough handled by W4019 – captained by Flight Lieutenant E. StC. Yeoman and another 10 Squadron 'boat, W3994, skippered by Pilot Officer Tom Egerton. Outward bound from the occupied French port of La Pallice, the *Luigi Torelli* was so badly mauled that it had to be beached at Santander in Spain.

PHILIP DAVIES COLLECTION

Victim... A Sunderland keeps guard as the armed merchant cruiser *Carinthia* lies disabled after a U-Boat attack off the west coast of Ireland, 7th June, 1940. *Carinthia*, the 20,277 ton ex-Cunard White Star passenger liner, was called up by the Admiralty for war duty as an auxiliary cruiser. It was torpedoed by Leutnant Engelbert Endrass' U-46 and remained afloat for some time before eventually sinking. Two officers and two ratings on the liner were killed but the rest of the crew, including Captain J. F. B. Barrett, were taken off safely. In the desperate early war days, the sight of disabled and sinking merchant vessels was an all so common sight for the crews of flying-boats.

FRED THOMAS

IV. WINGS OF PEACE

New kit... Personnel from 205 Squadron pose with the first of their new Sunderlands at Seletar, Singapore, September 1945. The squadron had converted from Catalinas at Koggala, Ceylon. Those identified are: Flt Lieut Tom Risk, Sqn Ldr Dunn, P/O Elliott, F/O Ken Jones, Tom Brewer, George Lee, Eddie Bradley-Fearey and Errol Oakley.

TOM BREWER

Fair dinkum!... Sunderlands from Seletar-based 209 Squadron flew the flag in Australia in 1949 and VB884 is seen over Brisbane. Too late for war service, VB884 was one of the last batch of Blackburn produced Sunderlands, and joined 209 Squadron in December, 1945. Its useful life ended in August, 1952, when it was struck off charge.

JIM MECKLEM

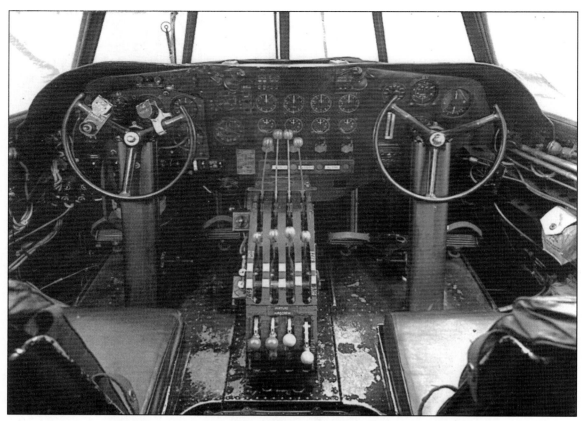

Seats of power... The 'office' of a Mark V Sunderland, a photograph which will stir many memories for anyone privileged to have sat in the 'hot seats' and flown the 'Queen of the 'Boats'.

ERIC MORTON

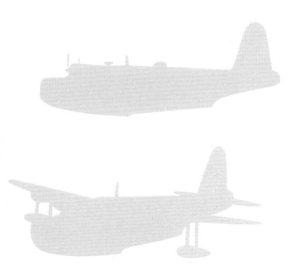

Cuppa up!... Skipper Flight Lieutenant 'Abe' Lincoln, cuppa in hand, lends support as one of the crew of ML797 carries out repairs at Malta, early 1957. ML797 was going 'down the line' to Singapore for the last time, to join 205/209 Squadron at Seletar.

BILL WHITER

Sights on home... Fitters and riggers of 230 Squadron soaking up the Seletar sunshine in late 1945. With the war in the Far East over, 230 Squadron – which had spent all its time from 1936 in overseas locations – returned to home waters in April, 1946. It was based at Castle Archdale, Calshot and, from 1949, at Pembroke Dock and was one of the last two UK squadrons to operate the mighty Sunderland.

D. RICHINGS

Pristine... New arrival RN284 takes on the 'Charlie' mantle with 201 Squadron at Pembroke Dock, August, 1945. A factory fresh Mark V, it was allocated to Flight Lieutenant Stan White and crew as replacement for a Mark III. RN284, another Dumbarton product, had a long and eventful career, serving twice with 201, and with 230 Squadron and 235 OCU. After the RAF had retired its UK based Sunderlands in 1957, RN284 went to the French Navy, being finally disposed of in January, 1962 – one of the very last of the famous breed.

HARRY TINDALE

Weatherworn... Appearances can be deceptive! A decidedly 'tatty' RN306 sits forlornly at Fanara, Egypt, waiting for repairs before flying on to the UK. Date is probably June, 1947. A Blackburn built Mark V, RN306 joined 205 Squadron in September, 1945, and later spent a long period in storage at Wig Bay. In 1953 it was one of 16 Sunderlands selected for the Royal New Zealand Air Force, being given the new serial NZ4118.

MRS CHRISTINA CROFT

Trainer... The much photographed SZ568 which gave sterling service as a trainer in the post-war RAF. Taken on charge in November, 1945, SZ568 had no operational status but served with 4 OTU (later 235 OCU) at Calshot before going into store in 1952. It was scrapped in October, 1956.

MRS DORIS McKAY

Goodwill... All set for their goodwill tour of the West Indies in 1951, these members of 201 Squadron look smart in their new issue uniforms. The naval officer next to 201's CO, Squadron Leader P. A. S. Rumbold, is US Navy Lieutenant Danny Decker on an exchange posting.

GIL CORP via KEN WILLIAMS

PD... RAF Pembroke Dock was the flyingboat man's 'Mecca', and was known to all 'webfooters' simply as 'PD'. The town and the Milford Haven Waterway were home base to flying-boats for nearly 30 years and Sunderlands operated from here for 19 of those years, 1938-57. This photograph was taken from Flight Lieutenant Comber's 230 Squadron Sunderland on 28th March, 1949. Almost exactly 10 years later the RAF Ensign would be lowered for the last time in the station, and 'PD' would pass into RAF history and webfooters' folklore.

MRS DORIS McKAY

Sub hunter... A peacetime view of EJ155, U-Uncle of 205 Squadron at Seletar. In its wartime days as a Mark III EJ155 tangled with a U-Boat when being flown by a crew from 330 (Norwegian) Squadron in July, 1944. U-387 was damaged and had to return to occupied Norway for repairs. Converted to Mark V status later on, EJ155 returned to active duty with 88 Squadron in the Korean War, subsequently joining 209 Squadron and then 205/209. It was pensioned off to the UK in November, 1955, and scrapped.

JOHN BERTOLA

Engine run... RN300 running up the starboard outer in its time with 209 Squadron at Seletar. Just too late for war service, RN300 served variously with 201, 209 and the joint 205/209 Squadrons before being struck off charge in April, 1957.

L. SCOTT via CHRIS ASHWORTH

Open sesame... Tower Bridge obligingly opens for PP115, A-C, of 201 Squadron which represented the RAF on the Thames for Battle of Britain Week, September, 1951. A Sunderland graced the Thames every September in the 1950s until the type was retired. The last military Sunderland to do Thames duty was DP198, also of 201 Squadron, in 1956. PP115 survived until being stuck off RAF charge in June, 1955.

ANDREW EDNEY

King, not Queen... Over a rural landscape PP163 of 235 OCU performs its unspectacular but necessary training duties, c1951. It carries the letter 'D' signifying 235 parentage, and the individual letter K for King. Built by Blackburns, PP163 served briefly at the war's end with 228 and 201 Squadrons. After lengthy storage it took up its trainer role in 1950 and by 1955 was with 230 Squadron. It went for scrap in October, 1957.

GERRY MORBEY

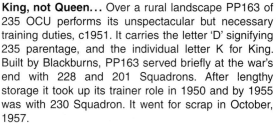

Finis... Looking like a stranded whale out of its natural element, war veteran JM667 awaits the inevitable at Seletar, 1954. JM667 started life as a Rochester built Mark III, being issued to the Norwegian manned 330 Squadron in March 1943. While in their hands as V-Victor it notched up a U-Boat sinking on 16th May, 1944, its victim being U-240. Conversion to Mark V standard, and lengthy periods of storage, were followed by service in the Far East with 209 and 205 Squadrons. It was struck off charge in October, 1954.

JOHN BERTOLA

Ploughman... Surrounded by attendant marine craft, Calshot-based Mark V EJ153 is prepared for slipping after a 'close shave' in June, 1951. While on a bombing training sortie, EJ153 came in a shade too low and skimmed the top of a hill, and the hull was pierced in several places. A safe alighting was made and the aircraft was run onto the beach. Afterwards it was nicknamed 'the Ploughman', from the furrow the hull made in the ground! EJ153 – which started life as a Windermere-built Mark III – served with 235 OCU at Calshot from 1949 until 1953. It later went to 230 Squadron and was struck off charge in November, 1956.

JOHN FIDLIN

Top left: Roadside stop at La Baule, Brittany, in the early 1970s was former French Navy Mark V, ML796, converted into a café and bar, complete with spiral staircase! Acquired by the Imperial War Museum in 1975, ML796 has been beautifully restored at Duxford, Cambridgeshire.
WING COMMANDER JOHN TIPTON

Bottom left: In their swansong days at Singapore, Sunderlands were still crowd pullers. Here ML797 of 205/209 Squadron – destined to be the last Sunderland to fly in the RAF – stars at a Seletar open day.
PETER M. THOMAS COLLECTION

Main picture: Memories are made of this – Pembroke Dock, c1956. Within months the Sun 20 years and flying boats – and 'PD' – would soc

Top right: Pembroke Dock's heritage on view within the walls of the former Royal Dockyard – the splendid sight of ML824 as a visitor attraction. Sadly, it only remained at 'PD' for a decade before being moved to Hendon Museum.
PETER M. THOMAS COLLECTION

Bottom right: End of the flight path for an anonymous 205/209 Squadron Sunderland at Seletar. To protect this lady's dignity the serial number has been removed but it could be NJ272.
BILL DAVIES

white-hulled Sunderlands at their moorings off
d left for the last time their Haven base of nearly
ust another chapter in RAF history.
JOHN HIRST

Supply mission... Fuel drums are ferried out to SZ581, Y-Yoke, of 230 Squadron at Greenland's Young Sound, during the 1952 re-supply of the British North Greenland Expedition. From Young Sound, Sunderlands made many missions to the Expedition's base camp on Britannia Lake, 200 miles away. Both 230 and 201 Squadrons from Pembroke Dock took turns in the short Arctic summers to fly in supplies for the scientists, and in 1954 the whole party was airlifted home by Sunderlands. SZ581 – built at Short's Belfast factory – served only with 230 Squadron throughout the late 1940s and early 1950s. It went into storage in 1954 and almost beat the scrapman, sinking at its Wig Bay moorings in November, 1955. It was salvaged and scrapped the following summer.

BILL WING

Mascot... Meet 'Kita', husky mascot of Pembroke Dock based 230 Squadron. Not always as docile as appearances show, 'Kita' was adopted by 230 after the Squadron brought the British North Greenland Expedition party back to Britain in 1954. The Expedition's huskies came too and as one of them was pregnant, 230 laid claim to the offspring. 'Kita' made quite an impression at Pembroke Dock, to say the least, and stayed on the Squadron's roll for a considerable time.

ROLAND MONTAGUE

Paying-off... ML797 gets a memorable send-off at it is hauled up the Seletar slipway for the last ever time, 22nd May, 1959. In good nautical tradition it flies a 'paying-off' pennant. Plans to preserve this venerable lady and fly it back to the UK came to nought, dealing RAF history a great disservice. For the record, ML797 was built at Shorts Rochester works and it spent time in the Far East after the war, although details are not clear. It joined 205/209 Squadron in March, 1957, and flew for the last time on 20th May, 1959. Officially, it was struck off charge on 30th June.

JACK POYSER

Farewell... to a mighty warrior. Aircrew and groundcrew of 205/209 Squadron pose for one last group photograph as an era ends with the retirement of the last Sunderlands in May, 1959. In the centre of the front row are Flight Lieutenants Ben Ford and Jack Poyser, co-pilot and pilot on the last flight made by an RAF Sunderland.

BILL WHITER

V. FILM STAR

A star at rest... Just another Sunderland perhaps but P9606 was very special, achieving star billing in the classic wartime film *Coastal Command*, premiered in London in October, 1942. *Coastal Command* – made by the Crown Film Unit – followed the fortunes of T for Tommy and its crew from their base somewhere on the Scottish coast. Preparations began in early 1941 but it was 18 months before cinemagoers were able to view the finished product. Ironically, by the time of its premiere, some of the flyingboat crew who starred in the film had been killed in action. They were lost in a 228 Squadron Sunderland, W4026, which crashed in Caithness, Scotland, on 25th August, 1942. Among those on board was HRH the Duke of Kent. As for P9606, it seems to have been plucked for stardom from the pool of Sunderlands at 4 OTU, Invergordon, which it joined in December, 1941. A Rochester built Mark I, it served first in 1940 with 10 Squadron, RAAF, at Mount Batten but was soon on 201 Squadron's strength. Coded ZM-R it made many Atlantic patrols with 201 up to August, 1941. With 4 OTU it took on the code combination TA-E as shown here. For its film role P9606 carried the codes DO-T, a somewhat confusing choice as 228 Squadron – which supplied some of the aircrew for 'Tommy' – had DQ as its codes. In OTU hands P9606 led a charmed life, surviving four minor mishaps. In one, two boat guards were injured when a match was struck, causing a small explosion. The one-time star of the big screen survived all the attentions of trainee crews, being finally pensioned off in May, 1944. At least two other Sunderlands appeared in the film. Briefly as 'understudy' was the third production Sunderland, L2160, which joined 4 OTU in April, 1942. And a 10 Squadron Mark I, coded RB-K, also made an appearance to help out 'Tommy' in one encounter with the Luftwaffe. This was possibly P9605 which came off the Shorts production line just before its sister. A slight questionmark is posed by one logbook which records 'Tommy' as being P9600. This aircraft, after service with 10 and 228 Squadrons, arrived at Invergordon in March, 1942. P9600 may, too, have masqueraded as the star of a film which remains a most evocative reflection of wartime flyingboat operations.

SQUADRON LEADER EDDY EDWARDS

Cameo role... P9605, which may have made a brief appearance in the film, pictured on its beaching gear at Mount Batten, Plymouth, wartime home of 10 Squadron, Royal Australian Air Force.

CAPTAIN VIC HODGKINSON

WORLD PREMIERE
of

COASTAL COMMAND

Produced with the full co operation of the Royal Air Force and the Royal Navy.

at the

PLAZA

THEATRE · PICCADILLY CIRCUS

FRIDAY OCTOBER 16TH

AT 7 P.M.
in aid of the

R.A.F. BENEVOLENT FUND

Programme... The cover of the programme for the world premiere of the film *Coastal Command*. Today the film is readily available on video.

BOB JONES

Film skipper... Smiles from two members of the crew of 'T for Tommy' in the film Coastal Command. Left is Wing Commander Ernest Leslie 'Johnnie' Hyde, DFC, who was captain of the aircraft, and with him is 228 Squadron's Pilot Officer Henry 'Tammy' Morton, DFM. Wing Commander Hyde was an experienced Sunderland pilot having served earlier in the war on 204 Squadron. After the filming was completed he returned to operational flying, taking command of a Beaufighter squadron at Dyce, Aberdeen. Sadly, within days he was killed on operations off the Norwegian coast and is buried at Trondheim, Norway. Morton, too, was lost on operations – in a 228 Squadron Sunderland which failed to return from patrol in January 1944. By then he had been promoted to Flight Lieutenant.

228 SQUADRON ARCHIVES

VI. FOREIGN FLAGS

Top: **Reworked...** Getting set for a new life in the Southern Hemisphere, one of 16 Mark V Sunderlands for the RNZAF is seen at Shorts, Belfast, where the aircraft were reconditioned in the early 1950s. The batch number under the cockpit includes the number 13, suggesting the 13th aircraft in the sequence. This would make it the former PP124, a Rochester built example, which did not see war service and only served with 205 Squadron before going into storage.

BILL MORTIMER COLLECTION

Upper Right: **Unwanted...** Engineless, tied down and wrapped up, NZ4118 awaits its fate at Hobsonville, alongside sisters in similar 'distress'. It is the former RN306 of RAF days. The Royal New Zealand Air Force withdrew its last Sunderland in April, 1967, having operated the type for 24 years.

Via MAP

Middle: **Springbok Daisy...** South African Air Force Sunderland 1710 being prepared at Congella, Durban, probably for its last flight – and the last flight by a Springbok Sunderland on 8th October, 1957. One of 16 ex-RAF Mark Vs operated by the SAAF between 1945 and 1957, 1710 was formerly RN281, a Blackburns example. Operated by 35 Squadron in South African service, 1710 carried the name 'Dynamite Daisy'. Worthy of preservation, it sadly went for scrap within weeks of its last flight.

SAAF MUSEUM

Bottom: **On the step...** All set for take-off is 1704 of the SAAF, seen here in the late 1940s. The former RN279, it saw brief war service with 461 Squadron, RAAF. With 35 Squadron, SAAF, it was given something of a mouthful of a name 'Umzinfirkin Fifi'. Like all its sisters, it was scrapped – 'Fifi's' demise being March, 1955.

SAAF MUSEUM

S'il vous plaît... The French operated Sunderlands for close on 20 years, from wartime use in Africa through to the early 1960s. Free French units based at Dakar and Bathurst – soon to become No 343 Squadron in the RAF – flew operationally for the last two years of the war. In November 1945, the Squadron was transferred to the Aeronavale, taking on French titling, with Dakar as the principal base. In war and peace, the French flew no less than 50 Sunderlands – Mark IIIs and Mark Vs – and the last two were pensioned off in January, 1962. Among a batch of 14 transferred from RAF stocks in 1951 was ML778, which began life as a Rochester-built Mark III. Wartime service in the hands of 422 RCAF, 228 RAF and 461 RAAF Squadrons was followed by upgrading to Mark V standard, complete with four Pratt and Whitney power plants. ML778 returned to active duty with 201 Squadron at Castle Archdale just as the war was ending. After VE-Day, patrols were continued for some weeks and it fell to ML778 to make the final official patrol of the war period, on 3rd/4th June, 1945, with 201's CO, Wing Commander Jackie Barrett, DFC, as skipper. New horizons beckoned with the transfer to the French Navy, but there was to be no happy ending for this war veteran. It was involved in a fatal accident in July, 1958, and was struck off the Navy's list in the September.

J. CUNY via CHAZ BOWYER

Back home... Settling back into old haunts at Pembroke Dock in March, 1961, ML824 is set for a long retirement. One of the last Sunderlands to be operated by the French Navy, ML824 flew on after its RAF sisters had been scrapped. Thankfully the French still had Sunderlands when a campaign started to preserve at least one of a famous wartime breed. The prime mover in the campaign was a West Wales farmer, Peter Thomas, and his tireless efforts were rewarded when ML824 was donated to the new Sunderland Trust, for preservation at Pembroke Dock. For a decade ML824, wearing the post-war code combination A - Z, was displayed at PD before it was reluctantly decided to transfer it to the newly established RAF Museum at Hendon in 1971. It is now on display in the Museum's Battle of Britain wing. In its early days, ML824 saw wartime service with 201 and 330 Norwegian Squadrons. It suffered the indignity of being struck off charge after the conflict but was not then scrapped and was returned to charge in 1948.

T. PRICE

Aloft... NZ4111 – former Blackburns built VB880 – shows its paces in New Zealand skies. This aircraft was scrapped in the mid-l960s, some time after being holed on rocks in the Chatham Islands.

NIGEL PERRY

New owners... What began as a straightforward transit flight from the UK to new battle grounds in West Africa took an unexpected turn for 95 Squadron's P9623. Newly transferred from 210 Squadron, with which it had carried the name 'The Lazy E', P9623 set off for Gibraltar but encountered bad weather off the coast of Portugal. The date was 14th February, 1941, and a cyclone which hit the coastline also snared up the lone Sunderland. Flight Lieutenant Evison and crew – including the flight commander, Squadron Leader Pat Lombard – were forced to land in territorial waters. The Portuguese authorities interned both Sunderland and crew but the RAF airmen were soon allowed to return. The Sunderland, though, was retained and later sold to Portugal. The photograph, taken soon after P9623's unexpected arrival on the Iberian Peninsula, shows the Sunderland being hoisted on to a barge crane at Tagus River, Lisbon.

ENG. MARIO CANONGIA LOPES

New markings… Portugal's newly acquired Sunderland was included in the country's naval aviation inventory and given the serial number 136. Flights over Lisbon, from the CAN (Aeronautical Naval Centre) of Bom Sucesso, Belem, were followed by a planned flight to Portuguese Guinea, An explosion in the starboard inner Pegasus led to the propeller tearing itself off, damaging the wing and the tips of the starboard outer propeller in the process. The outer engine had to be stopped and Captain Lieutenant Paulo Viana and his crew, in a fine exhibition of airmanship in a crippled machine, brought 136 back to Lisbon on the port engines only. This flight – on 8th March, 1944 – was the Sunderland's last and it was subsequently scrapped, The propeller-less engine and the damaged outer propeller are clearly seen in this photograph. By this time the aircraft was in bare metal finish with Portugal's 'Crosses of Christ' in red painted on the fuselage sides and wings. Green and red national flag colours adorn the full extension of the rudder.

ENG. MARIO CANONGIA LOPES

VII. HALF & HALF

Two into one... On a Pembroke Dock mooring in early 1944, G-George, an ASV festooned Mark III, waits for its next crew from 228 Squadron. It may not look anything out of the ordinary but DV980 was the unique 'Half & Half', made up of the fore and aft parts of two damaged aircraft. The story of George's 'reincarnation' is a remarkable one. On 1st June, 1943, when up slip for maintenance, DV980 came off its beaching trolley while being towed, damaging the rear hull and fuselage. Six days later another PD Sunderland, DV962, was badly damaged by fire, apparently while being cleaned with petrol. Two airmen were injured and the aircraft was not repairable. Instead of 'writing off' both airframes the idea of 'marrying' them up was mooted by Peter Newnham, who was in charge of the Short Brothers Working Party at Pembroke Dock, and it was he and his team who put theory into practice. The hulls were cut aft of the upper sloping deck, avoiding the bomb door aperture coamings, and DV962's aft part was mated with the front of DV980. The work took less than two months to complete and the 'new' DV980 was flight tested, found to be free from snags and immediately returned to active duty. The RAF had regained a serviceable Sunderland at a vital period of the maritime war, thanks to the ingenuity and first class workmanship of the Shorts team. To mark the aircraft's special story it was christened 'Half & Half' and a drawing of a foaming beer mug – half black, half white – was added to the nose, probably above the starboard door. No photographic record of this drawing appears to have survived.

MALCOLM ANDERSON

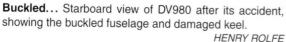

Buckled... Starboard view of DV980 after its accident, showing the buckled fuselage and damaged keel.

HENRY ROLFE

Scorched... The fire-ravaged mid section of DV962 after the disastrous fire on 7th June, 1943. The tail trolley is numbered 461, referring to the Australian squadron at Pembroke Dock. DV962 joined 202 Squadron in August, 1942, transferring to 119 Squadron soon after. In April, 1943, it went to 461 Squadron, and – minus its rear fuselage – was struck off charge in the August.

HENRY ROLFE

Creases... The fuselage of DV980 shows the results of parting from its beaching trolley. The hull was ruptured, causing a sagging and twisting through the rear section and the outer skinning and main structure were buckled. Yet within weeks 'George' was airborne again. A Rochester built Mark III, DV980 went first to 246 Squadron in October, 1942, joining 228 Squadron the following May. After its repair it flew many operations with 228. In one – on December 28th – Flight Lieutenant Gordon Lancaster and crew shadowed enemy destroyers and had a grandstand view of a naval engagement. The following February, DV980 was damaged in a night take-off at Pembroke Dock, hitting a large floating object which tore a hole in the hull. A successful landing was made in the daylight. DV980 had a charmed life, surviving five accidents. It later served with 423 Squadron, RCAF, at Castle Archdale, and was with 131 OTU at the end of the war. This unique warhorse was struck off charge within weeks of VE-Day.

HENRY ROLFE

VIII. CASUALTIES

Nose down!... A spectacular way to arrive on the holiday island of Guernsey for 201 Squadron's PP122. On a goodwill visit to its affiliated isle on 15th September, 1954, PP122 struck a submerged rock off St Peter Port and sank. The aircraft was recovered but never flew again, there being plenty of Sunderlands in storage to make up the loss. PP122 had a varied career with 461 RAAF, 10 RAAF and 201 Squadrons, plus time with the Anti-Submarine Warfare Development Unit.
201 SQUADRON ARCHIVES

Thar She Blows!... An undignified return to the surface for South African Sunderland 1706 after an accident at Congella on 13th April, 1950. The former RN305, it took up its new identity in October, 1945.
SAAF MUSEUM

Epic battle... Two soldiers stand guard at Praa Sands, near Marazion, Cornwall, on the wreck of EJ134, a Mark III of 461 Squadron, RAAF. In one of the classic encounters in the unceasing Battle of the Bay of Biscay, Flight Lieutenant Colin Walker and crew in EJ134 successfully fought off the challenges of six Junkers Ju88 long range Luftwaffe fighters. Flying from Pembroke Dock on 2nd June, 1943, Walker and crew were well into their patrol when the marauding fighters appeared. In a battle lasting 45 minutes, Walker's crew put up such stiff resistance that maybe four of their attackers were shot down. One of the Sunderland gunners was killed and several of the other crew injured. EJ134, riddled like a colander, still flew and brought its precious cargo back over the miles to landfall in Cornwall. Walker landed safely and rushed his sinking aircraft as near to the beach as possible. An amazing escape had just been effected. The Sunderland was quite intact after landing but tide and seas reduced it to a wreck by the next morning, pieces of the gallant aircraft being strewn over the sands. EJ134, built at Rochester, had joined 461 Squadron the previous December.

JOHN WITCOMB

From the deep... Emerging from the calm waters off the Pembroke Dock slipway in March, 1947, this Blackburn-built Mark V, VB886, will never fly again. It had a very short active life, joining 4 OTU at Pembroke Dock in October, 1946, and sinking in a gale on 16th March.

MRS DORIS McKAY

Going down... A sad finale for a mighty warrior as SZ599 prepares for its final plunge, being scuttled at Christmas Island in the Indian Ocean in 1954. The last-ever production Sunderland, SZ599 rolled off the Short and Harland line at Belfast in June 1946. It spent a lengthy time at MAEE, Felixstowe, before taking on squadron status with 205, 88 and 209 Squadrons in the Far East.

BILL MORTIMER COLLECTION

On a thread... The port float hangs precariously on PP117 of 201 Squadron during an exercise at Castle Archdale c1950. This resulted from a heavy landing but PP117 was saved and flew on through the 1950s, surviving until October, 1957, when it went for scrap.

FRED MARYON

Grounded!... Nosing up to the shore at Kai Tak, Hong Kong, in January, 1946, 209 Squadron's RN265 looks intact but was, in reality, a 'Category E' – a write-off. On take-off at Seletar, Singapore, the aircraft struck a ship's buoy, sustaining a huge gash in its hull. Flight Lieutenant McKendrick and crew completed the flight to Hong Kong where RN265 was successfully run ashore but it never flew again.

ROY EDMONDS

Up again... Back afloat after an unfortunate accident at China Bay, Ceylon, is M-Mike, a Mark V which hit a rock and sank while in transit from Singapore to Britain. The incident happened in 1950 or 1951 but 'Mike' has not yet been identified.

V. M. REEVE

Hulk... Almost unrecognisable as a section of a once beautiful Sunderland, a chunk of Mark I P9624 is broken up at Oban, following its crash on 15th March 1941. Returning at night from a convoy patrol, 210 Squadron's Flying Officer Derek Martin and crew met with a calm sea and hazy conditions and the aircraft crashed on landing. P9624 had had a very active war up to then, joining 210 Squadron the previous April. Often flown by a colourful character, Flying Officer (later Flight Lieutenant) Reggie Baker, P9624 made at least two attacks on Axis submarines – on 16th August 1940 and 6th January 1941 – one of which was credited at the time as a 'kill'. Baker commanded some stirring headlines in the national press at a time when there was precious little 'good news' to report, and he was awarded the DFC. By the time of D-Day in June 1944, Reggie Baker was commanding a wing of Typhoon fighters – a far cry from Sunderlands. An outstanding fighter leader, he was killed soon after D-Day during an attack in Normandy.

WING COMMANDER DEREK MARTIN OBE

Uplifted... An Admiralty lifting vessel lends a hand to take the mortal remains of P9602 from Lismore Island to Kerrera Island, off Oban, following a crash on 2nd September, 1940. This 10 Squadron, RAAF, aircraft was returning at night from a 12-hour convoy escort patrol and crashed into Lismore Island in bad weather.

WING COMMANDER DEREK MARTIN

Victim... The wreck of the seventh production Sunderland, L2164, after being attacked by Messerschmitt Bf 109s when moored at St Paul's Bay, Malta, 10th March, 1941. L2164 spent nearly all its time on 230 Squadron books and was one of three named in honour of the Federated Malay States Sultans in 1938, being christened 'Pahang'.

Via ANDY THOMAS

Gale havoc... A severe gale wreaked havoc amongst stored Sunderlands at the Wig Bay maintenance base in 1944, no less than 17 being blown over onto their port wing tips. Among them was Windermere-built Mark III DP198. It is seen here in the aftermath of the gale with port wing tip crumpled, port float broken and with its hull sitting on the wheels of a fractured beaching leg. The damage at Wig Bay kept Short Brothers teams busy for many months, each repair taking about six weeks. DP198 was fit and well again by September, 1944, and joined 423 Squadron, RCAF, in Northern Ireland. It returned to 57 MU, Wig Bay, when the war ended and was converted to a Mark V. From August 1950, it saw service with 209 and then 205 Squadrons in the Far East. In May 1956, it was issued to 201 Squadron at Pembroke Dock, and with the disbandment of the last UK-based Sunderland units DP198 went East again to Seletar, being one of the last two Sunderlands to fly in the RAF. It made its final flight in May, 1959, and was scrapped in Singapore.

HENRY ROLFE

Malta Dog... Storms, not sun at Malta as SZ570, recently with 88 Squadron, gets pounded at Kalafrana. A Belfast built Mark V, SZ570 joined 88 Squadron in March, 1946, taking the individual letter D - Dog. While staging through Malta en route to storage in the UK it was wrecked in this incident.

MRS DORIS McKAY

Stranded... Engine covers in place, 201 Squadron's W6055 awaits salvage efforts to commence at Benbecula in the Western Isles, late 1942. This was a particularly difficult operation for the Shorts Working Party and involved the construction of a temporary slipway to bring the aircraft ashore. The work took months to complete but W6055 flew again and later served with 330 Squadron. It went to storage at Wig Bay in March, 1944, and the 'plug' was pulled on its career when it was scuttled at the end of 1946.

HENRY ROLFE

Awash... In a sorry state at Mount Batten, Mark III DP179 receives the attentions of the salvage crew after running ashore when landing in bad weather. A 119 Squadron aircraft, coded V, DPI79 had completed a Bay of Biscay patrol on March 29th, 1943, and was diverted to Mount Batten. With cloud base at 500 feet a rapid downwind landing was made and the aircraft ran out of water. Flying Officer Cooke and crew smartly vacated the aircraft – one crewman jumping through a 'windmilling' propeller onto the ground below without being hurt! Salvaged by 10 Squadron personnel based at Mount Batten, DP179 was handed into the care of Shorts Working Party who worked their usual miracles and the Sunderland flew again. It joined 10 Squadron in August, 1943, and on 2nd October went missing on a Bay of Biscay patrol.

BILL STARK

Task ahead... The damaged planing bottom of DP179 after its accident at Mount Batten in March, 1943 – just one of the repairs needed before the aircraft could return to the water and the sky.

HENRY ROLFE

Afloat... but only just, 461 Squadron's PP116 is salvaged at Pembroke Dock, May, 1945. Just days after VE-Day, PP116 crashed on take-off, a sad ending to 461's long and successful association with PD. A new Mark V, PP116 was only issued to the Squadron on 14th February.

WALLACE DANN

Double trouble... DV958, a Rochester-built Mark III, was an unlucky 'boat. Within a matter of weeks in early 1943 it was twice badly damaged, and on both occasions it was repaired by Shorts Working Party. It is seen here at Pembroke Dock with damaged port wing and float after the aircraft broke its mooring and drifted onto rocks on 26th April, the hull sustaining damage too. This was just two days after DV958 had been returned to the water following repairs from a mishap on 26th January. In this incident, also at Pembroke Dock, the aircraft was approaching to land when the starboard engines failed at a height of 600 ft. A big bounce on landing removed the port float. At the time DV958 was with 119 Squadron but by October was back in action with 228 Squadron. Later it had spells at Calshot and with 10 Squadron, RAAF, before being issued to Scottish Aviation in December, 1944, perhaps for instructional purposes. A year later it was broken up at Killadeas, Northern Ireland.

HENRY ROLFE

Relic... Northern Ireland researcher James Stewart surveys a substantial relic of Mark III Sunderland DW110, which crashed on the Blue Stack Mountains, Co. Donegal, in the Irish Republic on 31st January 1944. For decades after the crash large pieces of the ill-fated flying boat remained, including the four Pegasus engines. DW110, of 228 Squadron based at Pembroke Dock, was diverted to Castle Archdale on return from patrol and hit a high peak in bad weather. Five out of the 12 crew survived.

Via JAMES STEWART

RIP... For many years this memorial reading RIP Airmen – has marked the crash site of DW110 in the Blue Stack Mountains, Eire. Seen here in 1986, it may now have faded even more. In recent years a plaque has been placed at the site in memory of the crew and their aircraft.

IAN PENTLAND

IX. BACK TO WAR

For the album... Within months of this photograph being taken many of these men from 88 Squadron, along with Sunderland ML882, were again on a war footing as the RAF became involved in the Korean conflict. New CO, Squadron Leader Mike Helme, is pictured with his new team in March or April, 1950. No 88 Squadron took on its flying-boat role in 1946 and served throughout the Korean War as well as taking part in the British operation against the Communist guerillas in Malaya. In these campaigns, 88 was joined by Sunderlands from 205 and 209 Squadrons, the aircraft adapting well to new tasks including bombing sorties. ML882 was no stranger to war, having joined 201 Squadron just before D-Day in 1944. Far Eastern service began with 88 Squadron in December, 1950, and it joined 209 Squadron in 1953. After returning to the UK a year later it was stored until going for scrap in October, 1956.

MRS CHRISTINA CROFT

Korean veteran... During the latter part of the Korean War RN293 saw service with both 209 and 88 Squadrons, later being transferred to the joint 205/209 Squadron at Seletar. It is seen here when with 88 Squadron, but also carried the letter 'F' with 209. It was disposed of in the Far East in late 1956.

Via CHRIS ASHWORTH

Malayan mission... Over a Malayan landscape, Belfast-built SZ566 keeps close station with two other Sunderlands. At the time it was either with 205 or 209 Squadrons. Between 1950 and 1954, SZ566 served in the Far East, latterly joining 88 Squadron. It ended its days as scrap metal in 1956.

V. M. REEVE

Second dickey... 88 Squadron Captain Fred Weaver had a VIP second pilot for his flight on 15th October, 1950 – Rear Admiral G. R. Henderson, United States Navy, the US Commander Fleet Air Japan. Flying RN277, Weaver and crew were detailed to fly to Inchon, Korea, and take the Admiral to Sasebo Kyushu.

SQUADRON LEADER FRED WEAVER

Strange bedfellows... A Sunderland crewman grabs some 'shut-eye' oblivious of his volatile companions. This photograph was probably taken on a mission over Malaya, the bombs being used against guerilla targets.

V. M. REEVE

To Japan... Against a stunning backdrop of islands, two Sunderlands return to their Japanese base at Iwakuni during the Korean War. Sunderlands ranged far and wide on a multitude of tasks during the war and provided an essential ferry service plus reconnaissance duties. Iwakuni is located beyond the headland below the leading aircraft.

MRS CHRISTINA CROFT

Rescue... A boatload of rescued airmen are about to find refuge in 205 Squadron's M - Mother, RN269. The story behind the photograph is not currently known but it is believed to show an incident which happened during the long-running Malayan campaign. What is known is that RN269 joined 205 Squadron in September, 1950, and was struck off charge in June, 1953. Earlier it had been with 201 Squadron. Information on the incident depicted would be welcome.

JOHN COOPER

Spoof... Clever darkroom techniques were employed to create this formation shot purporting to show five 88 Squadron Sunderlands near Japan's Mount Fuji. In reality, just two Sunderlands were returning on 21st August, 1951, from Yokosuka to Iwakuni, after a typhoon diversion. There is only one 'real' Sunderland in the frame, PP144.

MAURICE HURT

In company... B - Baker (NJ267) and C - Charlie (RN288) of 201 Squadron tuck in close, c1953. Both aircraft were to be lost in tragic accidents while with 201 Squadron. NJ267 crashed in the Milford Haven Waterway on 3rd March, 1954, and RN288 crashed off Eastbourne on 4th June, 1955, while 'flying the flag' for the RAFA Conference being held in the town.

MRS R. M. WILLMOTT

Return ticket... The four Sunderlands bringing the British North Greenland Expedition team home from the Arctic North sweep low over the Pembroke Dock waterfront before landing, August, 1954. The aircraft, flown by 230 Squadron crews, included VB889, D - Dog, borrowed from 201 Squadron and which, most appropriately, was carrying the contingent of huskies which were also brought back.

GROUP CAPTAIN J. W. LOUW

Left: **From below...** Part of 205 Squadron's Anniversary fly past, c1955. Leading is RN300 with SZ577 to starboard and RN278 to port.

V. M. REEVE

Below left: **Queen's salute...** Sunderlands from 201 and 230 Squadrons practice for the special aerial tribute to Her Majesty prior to the Queen's visit to Pembrokeshire in August, 1955. Leading are 230 Squadron's foursome of PP163 (Squadron Leader 'Red' Stavert), JM718, ML817 and SZ560. Tucking in behind are 201's formation.

JOHN LEEKS

Below: **Home run...** Mark III Sunderlands of 461 Squadron, RAAF, set course over Southern England for Pembroke Dock, sometime in 1943. Three aircraft had the previous day diverted to Mount Batten, Plymouth, due to bad weather. Nearest aircraft was being flown by Squadron Leader A. G. 'Rich' Richmond, RAAF.

SQUADRON LEADER A. G. RICHMOND
via MRS MARGARET BLACK

Vantage... A remarkable view indeed of six Sunderlands – from 201 Squadron – in formation during wartime. This shot was taken from a rooftop vantage at RAF Lough Erne, Northern Ireland (later to be re-named RAF Castle Archdale) on 1st December 1941. All the aircraft in this line-up have been identified though it is not known in which 'pecking order' they appear. It is thought that Flight Lieutenant Fleming DFC was leading in W3988, ZM-P, along with W3977, ZM-Q (Flt Lieut Smith); P9604, ZM-S (Flt Lieut Fletcher); W3981, ZM-W (Flt Lieut Raban); T9077, ZM-Y (Flt Lieut Spink), and L2168, ZM-Z (Flying Officer Powell). Also aloft at this time was another 201 Squadron aircraft, T9084, flown by Flight Lieutenant Cooper. Just two days later W3988 was lost in a crash near Carrowmore Point, County Clare, Eire, and W3977 was a casualty the following February, crashing in the sea off Donegal.

RAYMOND HARTSHORN

Head on... A classic view of magnificent machines seen through the camera lens of Master Engineer Vim Reeve. Slight variations to radio and radar fits mark these out as New Zealand operated versions, on exercise with the RAF at Seletar, probably around March, 1956.

V. M. REEVE

Above Top: **Follow the leader...** The new generation of land-based maritime reconnaissance aircraft follow in the wake of 201 Squadron's SZ575 in this special formation which flew over several UK locations in 1955. Following behind are (left) an American-built Lockheed Neptune, and an Avro Shackleton. The Shackleton was to finally displace the Sunderland in maritime roles in the late 1950s. For the record, SZ575 joined 201 Squadron in February, 1955, remaining with the unit until it disbanded in early 1957. The aircraft was scrapped the following October.
SQUADRON LEADER ALAN NICOLL

Above Bottom: **Beat up...** Fast and low by Squadron Leader P. A. S. Rumbold, CO of 201 Squadron, and Flight Lieutenant Jack Ramsden as they and their crews arrive in Bermuda for a goodwill visit, July 1951.
KEN WILLIAMS

Left: **Full power...** as a 205 Squadron duo race over the water at Seletar. They were participating in a formation to celebrate the squadron's 25th anniversary on flying-boats.
V. M. REEVE

Trio... Three new Mark Vs in formation, though their unit is not known. They may be new equipment for 230 Squadron, based at Koggala, Ceylon.
WING COMMANDER DUNDAS BEDNALL

XI. IN CIVVIES

Trials... Carrying the temporary British registration G-AGPZ, Sandringham II *Argentina* is about to get airborne on a test flight prior to delivery to its new owners in Buenos Aires. A conversion carried out by Short and Harland in Belfast, G-AGPZ began life as a Mark III Sunderland, DD834, which saw operational service with 204 and 228 Squadrons. Its conversion included the fitting of Pratt and Whitney Twin Wasps and accommodation for 28 passengers on the lower deck and 17 on the upper. Launched on 17th November, 1945, the Sandringham was soon on its way to South America, operating with the registration LV-AAP between cities on the River Plate. In July 1948, it was written off in a crash at Buenos Aires.

SHORT AND HARLAND via ERIC ODDY

Speedbird... Carrying the Speedbird motif of BOAC, the RAF Transport Command codes OQZF and its original military serial number ML788, the one and only Sandringham I taxies past. Originally a Mark III Sunderland, ML788 returned after war service to Shorts at Rochester for full airliner conversion. Nose and tail turrets and fairings were removed and the 'new look' nose profile added. Retaining its Pegasus radials, it was fitted with two decks with seats and berths for 24 day or 16 night passengers on the lower deck with a dining saloon and bar above. Re-launched in November, 1945, it returned to BOAC the following June and operated with the airline until transferred to Aquila in 1949, and was scrapped soon after. It operated mostly with the civil registration G-AGKX and the name *Himalaya*.

ERIC ODDY

Pioneer... Sunderlands joined their 'Empire' class sisters on civilian routes in March, 1943, the first six – JM660 - JM665 – being converted off the Rochester line. With BOAC they initially operated a regular service from Poole to Lagos, Nigeria. JM665/W is seen here at Kasfareet, Egypt. The civilian registration G-AGEW was allocated but for a time JM665 operated with the RAF Transport Command military coding OQZW. It carried the name *Halton* with BOAC, later changed to *Hanwell*. G-AGEW survived the war and was written off in an accident in September, 1948.

RAF MUSEUM P10274

Camouflage... Awaiting its next wartime flight is G-AGHZ, one of the second batch of Mark III Sunderlands allocated to BOAC in 1943. For their wartime role the Sunderlands carried standard RAF camouflage with the black lettering outlined in silver and red, white and blue underscoring. The former ML727, 'HZ carried the name *Hastings* and, later, *Hawkesbury*. After its BOAC career it went to Aquila Airways in 1949 and was scrapped at Hamble three years later.

REAL PHOTOGRAPHS / MAP

Hythe... Seen at Hamble awaiting the scrapman, G-AGJM deserved a better fate. Initially ML754 on the Rochester line, it joined BOAC in February, 1944. With the return of peace, BOAC upgraded their Sunderlands to full airliner standard, removing the austerity bench and mattress seating. G-AGJM was the first to be completed, receiving the name *Hythe* which also became the class name. The Hythe-class retained the nose and tail turret fairings of their military sisters. In an epic survey flight beginning on 17th February, 1946, Captain R. C. Parker flew *Hythe* – with BOAC Chairman Lord Knollys aboard – from Poole to Australia, New Zealand, Hong Kong, Shanghai and Tokyo. In 206 hours actual flying time, *Hythe* covered over 35,000 miles, becoming the first British civil flyingboat to visit China and Japan. Its BOAC service ended in February, 1949, when it went to Aquila Airways, Britain's last civilian flyingboat operator. In January, 1952, G-AGJM was scrapped at Hamble.

MAP 016352

Airlift... *Hampshire*, one of the original Mark III Sunderlands operated by BOAC, is seen at Hamble in the late 1940s when with Aquila Airways. Originally JM663, it joined BOAC in January, 1943, as G-AGEU. Aquila purchased 'EU in 1948 and flew it on the early stages of the Berlin Airlift. Withdrawn from use in March, 1953, it was scrapped the following August.

PETER MERRETT

Fjord queen... Norway was another operator of Sandringhams, five being registered in the late 1940s. They flew in and around the fjords and retained the radar equipment of Mark V Sunderlands as an aid. The starboard radar scanner housing can be seen on LN-IAV, the one-time ML809, a Mark III which saw no war service. Sold to the makers in 1946, it became a Sandringham VI and adopted the name *Kvitbjorn* with Norwegian airline DNL. Operating always in difficult areas, 'IAV did not have a long career, crashing at Tjelesund in August, 1947.

REAL PHOTOGRAPHS / MAP

XII. ML814

Military days... As a Mark III Sunderland, ML814 saw wartime service with 201 and 422 RCAF Squadrons at Pembroke Dock in 1944, being converted to Mark V standard in early 1945. It was later used by the Norwegian-manned 330 Squadron from Sullom Voe and from Sola in Norway. Like so many other Sunderlands, ML814 went into long term storage in 1946 and in 1953 was one of the 16 aircraft chosen for re-build for the Royal New Zealand Air Force. In June, 1954, with the new serial NZ4108, the Sunderland arrived in Fiji but it had a short career with the RNZAF. It was stored in 1957 and was purchased six years later by the Australian airline Ansett. NZ4108 is seen on a trial flight before the RNZAF took it on charge.

SHORT BROTHERS

Role supreme... This splendid sight was all too soon lost to British eyes as the one-time ML814 – the world's last airworthy Sunderland – flew away to take up residence in the USA in 1993. The aircraft, registered G-BJHS, returned to the UK from the Virgin Islands in March 1981 having been purchased by Mr Edward Hulton. With flag flying proudly, it is seen carrying the name *Sir Arthur Gouge* after Short Brothers' brilliant Chief Designer. Looking out of the first pilot's window is Ken Emmott who flew Catalinas in the RAF and later was a captain on flying-boats with BOAC. Ken Emmott piloted 'the last Sunderland' for much of the final decade when it was UK-based, surely the 'role supreme' for any 'Webfooter'? After being acquired by American collector Kermit Weeks the Sunderland was flown across the Atlantic and today is displayed at 'Fantasy of Flight' in Florida.

Via KEN EMMOTT

Islander... For 10 years, from October 1964, the now much-changed ML814 carried out a regular service in Australia between Rose Bay and Lord Howe Island. Converted in Australia, it acquired a more rounded nose profile than its sister Sandringhams so remained a civilian Sunderland. Seen here in 1970 with the titling Ansett Flying Boat Services and the Australian registration VH-BRF, it was named, appropriately, *Islander*. When Ansett pensioned off its two Shorts flying-boats, both were bought by Captain Charles Blair of Antilles Air Boats, for operation in the Virgin Isles. In the event the now re-named *Excalibur VIII* was only stored at San Juan and was rescued from there by Edward Hulton.

MAP 045675

Salute... Sporting new titles and a new name, *Spirit of Foynes*, the last flying Sunderland beats up Gatwick Airport's runway in July 1989. The Ryan Air titles were part of an arrangement which took the aircraft to Ireland in August 1989, but it returned to the old flying-boat station at Calshot soon after and remained there until making the epic flight to the United States.

GATWICK AIRPORT

Calamity... For a number of years the Sunderland – now registered G-BJHS – was based at Chatham and was set to fly on 16th October, 1987, to celebrate the 50th anniversary of the first Sunderland flight. Disaster struck when the gale force winds which devastated parts of southern England caught up the Sunderland and toppled it from its tail trolley, severely damaging the starboard wing. There were fears that the aircraft would never fly again but a deal with the Imperial War Museum at Duxford saw the transfer of part of the wing of their static airframe, ML796, for grafting onto the Sunderland. Duxford's Sunderland had the repaired but non-airworthy wing parts in return. G-BJHS looks rather forlorn at Chatham in the Autumn of 1988, the wing repairs proceeding slowly.

HENRY ROLFE

XIII. MEMORIES

Sweeping in... SZ567, starboard outer stopped, sweeps in over the Wig Bay facility in 1954 at the time of the handover of the last of the 16 Sunderlands to the Royal New Zealand Air Force. The display pilot was Fred Weaver.
SQUADRON LEADER FRED WEAVER

Look out!... A so-close view of a 95 Squadron 'boat as it bears down on another Sunderland in West African skies.
WING COMMANDER VINCE FURLONG

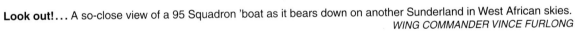

Two down... and two still running. Proof, if it was needed, that a Mark V Sunderland would quite happily stay aloft with two engines feathered. Indeed, it would do so on one engine only! An air day special by 201 Squadron's B-Baker in the 1950s.

JOHN BISHOP

Victory... An unique aerial formation to celebrate victory over Japan was staged by 240 Squadron over Madras in October, 1945. Wing Commander Gavin-Robinson leads an 11-aircraft formation. The other Sunderlands were skippered by F/O Banton, F/O Robinson, F/Lt Goulborn, W/O Nears, W/O Monk, F/O Edwards and F/O Coy, while the three 'special duty' Catalinas were captained by F/Lt McColl, F/Lt Myers and F/Lt Beaumont.

MAX BEAUMONT

KIPPER FLEET CARTOONS

Poster... A sub-spotting Sunderland featured in an aircrew training poster, created by Corporal Arthur Banks, 259 Squadron, Dar-es-Salaam, 1945.

DR ARTHUR BANKS

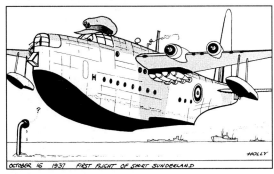

Cap that!... A superior looking Sunderland in a cartoon by Holly to mark the type's 50th anniversary, October 1987.

CHARLES HALL

En garde... Kane, who served on Sunderlands in the Far East in the 1950s, produced a series of splendid 'Kipper Fleet' cartoons, two of which are depicted here. 'En garde' obviously refers to the motto of 88 Squadron.

Via J. A. WILSON

All aboard!... Wing Commander I. G. Oakley-Beuttler's classic cartoons graced the pages of *The Tatler*. Here he turns his attentions in 1939 to the new fangled Sunderland, then entering service.

Via CAPTAIN VIC HODGKINSON

Xmas gifts... A Sunderland gets Christmas presents from a Dakota in a four foot square mural created by Corporal Arthur Banks in 1944, for an RAF island base in the Indian Ocean.

DR ARTHUR BANKS

Inspection... Reg Gill's memories of 204 Squadron Sunderlands at Sullom Voe in 1940 obviously included the frustrations of carrying out maintenance and inspections on the water!

Via REG GRAHAM